Sikh
holy days

KT-444-784

Worshippers watch an outdoor procession.

993079745 9

Glossary

AKHAND PATH A ceremony used to celebrate many Sikh holy days. During an akhand path the entire Guru Granth Sahib is read out loud non-stop in the gurdwara.

BAPTISM This is a ceremony practised in several different religions which confirms a person's faith or marks their entry into the faith. In Sikhism, people must choose to be baptised when they are adults.

CREMATE In many places, when people die the custom is to burn the bodies instead of burying them. This is called cremation.

FIVE BELOVED The first five Sikhs to be baptised, and the first members of the Khalsa. They are also called the Panj Piares.

FORTY IMMORTALS Forty men who gave their lives in order to save the life of Guru Gobind Singh.

GOLDEN TEMPLE The holiest Sikh gurdwara and shrine, located in Amritsar, India. The Golden Temple is actually a complex of many buildings.

GURDWARA The Sikh house of worship.

GURU A wise person or leader. The Sikh Gurus are the first ten men who led the Sikhs during the beginning of Sikhism. Guru Nanak was the first Sikh Guru and Guru Gobind Singh was the last living Guru.

GURU GRANTH SAHIB The holy book of Sikhism. Sikhs consider the book to be the last Sikh Guru.

GURUPURAB A day that celebrates or remembers important events in the lives of the Sikh Gurus and the Sikh community.

HYMN A song with a religious meaning.

KHALSA The worldwide group of baptised Sikhs. Any Sikh adult can become a member of the Khalsa by going through the baptism ceremony. The members of the Khalsa are responsible for following Sikh ideals.

LANGAR A free kitchen in the gurdwara. Sharing a meal in the langar is a part of worship. On holy days, Sikhs also offer food to anyone who comes to a Sikh festival and they use the langar to help feed people of any religion who are in need.

LUNAR CALENDAR A calendar based on the phases of the Moon. The Hindu calendar is lunar and the dates of some Sikh holy days are calculated on the lunar calendar.

MARTIAL Another word for military or for fighting. Martial skills are skills that may be used in fighting.

MOGHULS The people who ruled India at the time of the beginning of Sikhism. The Moghuls were Muslims.

NAGAR KIRTAN A procession held on some holy days, when the Guru Granth Sahib is brought out of the gurdwara and paraded around the neighbourhood, usually followed by musicians and people carrying Sikh flags.

NISHAN SAHIB The Sikh flag. It is flown outside gurdwaras as a way to signal that a building is a gurdwara. It may also be carried during processions.

PUNJAB A part of modern day India where Sikhism began.

SOLAR Another word for Sun. A solar calendar is one that is based on the way the Earth moves around the Sun.

Contents

As you go through the book, look for words in **BOLD CAPITALS**. These words are defined in the glossary.

⚠ Understanding others

Remember that other people's beliefs are important to them. You must always be considerate and understanding when studying about faith.

A worship service in a gurdwara.

What is a holy day?

Sikh holidays celebrate important events in the history of the Sikh religion.

People of all faiths worship throughout the whole year. But in all faiths, some days are special. These special days, or holy days, may remember an important event in the history of the faith, or they may be written about in holy writings, or scripture.

Different holy days

These holy days are different from a day of rest and worship that many religions have each week. Many holy days involve public celebrations, special meals, festivals and even processions. In general, we call these special days holy days and it is from this that we get the word 'holiday'.

Whereas Muslims reserve Friday as a special day, Jews Saturday and Christians Sunday, in the Sikh faith, there is no special weekly day of rest. Many Sikhs worship in the gurdwara one or more times each week. But there are also many holy days and times throughout the year, each with its own name. These days and times celebrate or remember important events in the history of the Sikh faith.

▲ Sikh worshippers bow in front of the GURU GRANTH SAHIB during worship.

Sikh and Hindu holy days

Some Sikh holy days have the same name, and happen on the same day, as Hindu holy days.

Many of the first Sikhs came from Hindu families and had been Hindus. So the new Sikh leaders kept the Hindu holy days as holidays but changed their meaning. So, in this book, you will read about both the Hindu and Sikh holidays.

Sikhism began in the part of India called the PUNJAB and this is still where most Sikhs live. So, although Sikhs all over the world celebrate holy days, the largest celebrations take place in Punjab. In the UK, the celebrations may be smaller and simpler, but they are just as important for the people taking part.

As you look at the main holy days of the Sikh faith in this book, notice how each day is marked out or celebrated in a different way. Some holy days remember happy events, such as the birthday of one of the founders of Sikhism; while other holy days remember sad days, such as the day an important Sikh died. But all of these days are reminders of Sikh beliefs and faith.

Weblink: www.CurriculumVisions.com

The Sikh holy calendar

Here are the parts of the year when Sikh holidays occur. The actual date varies from one year to another.

To keep track of the days of the year, many people in the world use a calendar which divides the year into 12 months and begins on January 1. In this calendar, the Sun is used as a guide and one year is about the time it takes the Earth to move around the Sun.

But not all calendars look like this. Some calendars, for example, use the way the Moon moves across the sky as a guide. So, the holy days move around a little each year.

The Sikh calendar uses both ways. When Sikhism began, it used the Hindu calendar, which is based on the Moon.

The Sikh Calendar	
Chet	March 14
Vaisakh	April 14
Jeth	May 15
Harh	June 15
Sawan	July 16
Bhadon	August 16
Asu	September 15
Katik	October 15
Maghar	November 14
Poh	December 14
Magh	January 13

▲ Each new month in the Sikh calendar begins on or near the New Moon.

▼ On holy days, free food is handed out to worshippers.

Later, the Sikh calendar was changed to one that is based on the Sun, but some of the holy days are still calculated using the Hindu calendar and so they change from year to year.

► In this chart, you can see how the Sikh holy days are spread around the year. You can also see how some of the holidays (based on the Moon) move around a little from year to year while others (based around the Sun) do not.

SIKH HOLY DAYS

	2007	2008	2009	2010	2011
Hola Mohalla	Mar 4	Mar 22	Mar 11	Mar 1	Mar 20
Vaisakhi	Apr 14	Apr 14	Apr 14	Apr 14	Apr 14
Diwali	Nov 9	Oct 28	Oct 17	Nov 5	Oct 26
Maghi	Jan 13	Jan 13	Jan 13	Jan 13	Jan 13
Guru Nanak day	Apr 14	Apr 14	Apr 14	Apr 14	Apr 14
Guru Singh day	Jan 5	Jan 5	Jan 5	Jan 5	Jan 5

In 1998, Sikhs switched from a LUNAR CALENDAR, where holidays moved around, to using fixed dates for some of the holidays. Other holidays still use the lunar calendar and move every year.

Hola Mohalla

This holy day celebrates the Sikh ideal of always being prepared to help others.

The first month of the Sikh year is called Chet. It begins in March. Hola Mohalla is celebrated at the beginning of Chet, one day after Hindus celebrate Holi. Because of this, the date of Hola Mohalla changes each year.

The first Hola Mohalla

When Sikhism began, many Sikhs came from Hindu families and many of these Sikhs still celebrated some of the Hindu holidays, like Holi. In Hinduism, Holi is a joyous holiday that celebrates the arrival of spring.

▼ Every year in Anandpur, India, and around the world, Sikhs celebrate Hola Mohalla with pretend battles and tests of riding, archery and other military exercises.

At that time, Sikhism was led by wise people called **GURUS**. The tenth Guru, Guru Gobind Singh decided that Sikhs should celebrate Sikh ideals, so he created the three-day holiday of Hola Mohalla as a separate Sikh holy time.

This all happened hundreds of years ago, when the Sikhs were fighting the **MOGHUL** people, who ruled over most of India and Pakistan.

So Guru Singh decided that Hola Mohalla would be celebrated by a gathering of Sikhs for military exercises and 'mock' battles. These exercises would remind Sikhs of the important ideals of bravery, and of always being ready to defend yourself and others.

The first Hola Mohalla festival was celebrated in Anandpur, the home of Guru Singh. Today, Sikhs all over the world celebrate Hola Mohalla wherever they live.

Celebrating Hola Mohalla

Wherever it is celebrated, Hola Mohalla begins with early morning prayers at the GURDWARA and a communal meal in the LANGAR.

Throughout the three-day holiday, there may be processions through the streets and neighbourhoods around gurdwaras. These may include handing out free sweets and other foods (langar) and music.

In the gurdwaras there may also be special worship services where people can hear religious talks, stories and poems about Guru Gobind Singh and other brave Sikhs.

Martial contests

During the first Hola Mohalla, Guru Singh formed a Sikh army called the Nihang Singhs, to protect Sikhs and others. So, in some places, Hola Mohalla celebrations include MARTIAL contests and demonstrations of ancient fighting skills such as archery, sword fencing, horse riding, tent pegging, bareback horse-riding, standing upright on two speeding horses and shooting. There may also be mock battles. These are all for fun, and care is taken to make sure that no one is hurt.

Even though Sikhs do not have to fight for their survival any more, the battles are a reminder of the Sikh ideal to always be prepared to defend yourself and others.

Other ways to celebrate

Hola Mohalla is also a time for music and poetry competitions. On the last day of the holiday, there is a long procession.

◀ Hola Mohalla begins with worship services at the gurdwara.

◄▲ Traditional music and processions through the streets around the gurdwara are often a part of Hola Mohalla celebrations.

Vaisakhi, the Sikh New Year

This day celebrates the founding of the Khalsa and the New Year.

The holy day of Vaisakhi, on April 14, is called the Sikh New Year, because, until recently, this day was the first day of the Sikh calendar. Even though the calendar has changed, Vaisakhi is still thought of as the New Year holiday. So, for Sikhs, this day celebrates both the start of a new year, and a new start for the Sikh faith. It is sometimes called the birthday of the **KHALSA**.

As with other Sikh holidays Vaisakhi began as a Hindu holiday – the Hindu New Year. For Hindus, this day is a time to celebrate the harvest season and to worship the Hindu goddess Durga.

The story of Sikh Vaisakhi and the Khalsa

On April 13, 1699, Guru Gobind Singh called all the Sikh leaders to the city of Anandpur, in the Punjab area of India. He then asked all the people there who was willing to die for their faith.

Eventually, one person stepped forward. The Guru took this volunteer behind a screen, the crowd heard a thud, and the Guru came back out with his sword dripping with blood. Four more men volunteered, and the same thing happened each time.

Finally, Guru Singh went behind the screen for a long time. Then he came out, followed by the five men, who were now dressed in saffron-coloured clothing. The five men were alive after all – the Guru had killed five goats instead. It was a test to select the most loyal and devout Sikhs.

After this, Guru Singh announced that these men would be the first five members of the Khalsa, or group of baptised Sikhs. Guru Singh then baptised the five men by giving each one a drink of sugar water, called amrit, that he had specially prepared and blessed. These first five members of the Khalsa are called the Panj Piares, or the FIVE BELOVED.

Then Guru Singh baptised the other Sikh leaders as members of the Khalsa. The men were given the new surname of Singh, which means 'lion' or 'lion-hearted'; and baptised women were given the new surname of 'kaur', which means princess.

Weblink: www.CurriculumVisions.com

▲ These Sikhs are
celebrating Vaisakhi
at an outdoor festival
by dancing traditional
Punjabi dances.

◀ These people are handing out
free food at an outdoor festival.

Celebrating Vaisakhi

Because Vaisakhi is the day the first Sikhs were baptised, many Sikhs choose to be baptised on Vaisakhi. So, there are **BAPTISM** ceremonies at most gurdwaras.

Outside each gurdwara is a Sikh flag, called the **NISHAN SAHIB**, on a flag pole. The flag pole is wrapped in a saffron-coloured cloth. On Vaisakhi, this cloth is taken down and a clean, new cloth is wrapped around the flag pole.

After these ceremonies, there are worship services in the gurdwara. In some places, the Guru Granth Sahib is carried in a procession around the ncighbourhood. The processions may also include bands playing Sikh religious music, people handing out food, people singing **HYMNS** and traditional dances.

▼ These people are playing traditional music at a Vaisakhi celebration in Trafalgar Square, London.

Weblink: www.CurriculumVisions.com

Diwali, a day of freedom

This holy time celebrates several different events in Sikh history.

The festival of Diwali is celebrated on the fifteenth day of the Sikh month of Katik (October/November).

The word Diwali means 'rows of lighted lamps' and the celebration is also called the Festival of Lights because one way that Hindus celebrate is by lighting small oil lamps and placing them around the home, in courtyards and in gardens, as well as on roof-tops and outer walls. The lights are to welcome the Hindu gods and goddesses into people's homes.

However, for Sikhs, this holiday has a different meaning. Many of the early Sikhs had converted from Hinduism and they still wanted to celebrate on Diwali. But Sikhism does not believe in worshipping gods and goddesses. So the Sikh Gurus changed Diwali into a time for gathering to worship God.

Sikhs also light lamps on Diwali, just like Hindus. But for Sikhs, the lights are not to welcome gods and goddesses. Instead, the lights are a reminder of the importance of being able to worship God.

They are also a reminder of the Sikh belief that God brings the light of truth into the world.

The Golden Temple

In 1577, the Sikhs laid the very first foundation stone for the **GOLDEN TEMPLE** at Amritsar, India, on Diwali. So, after this, Diwali became a day for Sikhs to celebrate the building of the Golden Temple, which is the centre of the Sikh faith.

But many years later, Sikhs had another reason to celebrate Diwali.

▲ This archway leads to a walkway that takes worshippers into the Golden Temple.

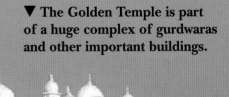

▼ The Golden Temple is part of a huge complex of gurdwaras and other important buildings.

The story of Sikh Diwali

Remember that, when Sikhism began, India was ruled by Muslim Emperors and was called the Moghul Empire. The Moghul rulers did not like the Sikhs, because they were afraid that the Sikhs would challenge their power.

In 1619, the Emperor Jahangir put the sixth Sikh Guru, Guru Hargobind, in jail. Fifty-two Hindu leaders were also in jail with Guru Hargobind. The Hindu leaders were also people the Emperor was afraid of. They were all imprisoned in a fort in the town of Gwalior.

Eventually, some Moghul leaders who were friends of Guru Hargobind convinced the Emperor to release him. But Guru Hargobind refused to be released unless the Hindu leaders were also set free.

Emperor Jahangir told the Guru that he would free any Hindu prisoners who could hold onto the Guru's coat tails while he walked out of prison. The Emperor thought that only five or six people would be able to hold onto Guru Hargobind's coat tails. But Guru Hargobind had a special coat made and brought to him in prison. This coat had 52 tails and so every one of the Hindu leaders was set free. After this the Hindu leaders gave Guru Hargobind the name Bandi Chhor, which means 'deliverer from prison'.

After he was released from prison, Guru Hargobind went to the Punjab, to worship at the Golden Temple in Amritsar. He arrived there on the day of Diwali. In thanks for the Guru's release, the gurdwara was lit with hundreds of Diwali lamps. After this, Sikhs called Diwali, Bandi Chhor Diwas, the 'day of freedom'.

▲ The Golden Temple lit up for Diwali.

What Diwali means to Sikhs

The story of Guru Hargobind is a reminder of some important Sikh beliefs. One of these is the freedom to worship and observe your faith, no matter what you believe.

Guru Hargobind was put into jail because he argued that the Muslim Emperor was being unkind to non-Muslims in India.

Guru Hargobind believed that all people should be treated equally. Guru Hargobind then refused to leave the prison without the Hindu leaders. This shows the Sikh respect for all other faiths.

The Guru was also willing to risk his life to help others, which is another very important part of Sikh beliefs.

▼ On Diwali, thousands of Sikhs celebrate by lighting candles outside and around the Golden Temple in Amritsar.

Celebrating Sikh Diwali

When Guru Hargobind returned to Amritsar after he was released from jail, he was welcomed by thousands of Sikhs. The Golden Temple was lit up with Diwali lamps to welcome the Guru home. Today, Sikhs continue this tradition by lighting lamps on Diwali each year. The lamps are a reminder of the Sikh ideal of always trying to help others, the way that Guru Hargobind helped the Hindu leaders. In Amritsar, the Golden Temple is lit up with thousands of lights and lamps. There may also be firework displays.

Wherever they live, many Sikhs go to the gurdwara to worship on Diwali. The worship services may include a talk about the story of Guru Hargobind.

On Diwali, people also give gifts of sweets to friends and relatives. This is a reminder of the sweetness of freedom.

Maghi

This holiday remembers the sacrifice of a brave group of Sikhs.

The holiday of Maghi is another holiday that is shared by Hindus (who call it Lohri) and Sikhs. It falls on the first day of the month of Magh (January).

The Sikh holiday of Maghi celebrates an event that happened in 1705, when Guru Gobind Singh was the leader of the Sikhs. At this time, Sikhs were still fighting the Moghul Emperor.

The story of Maghi

In December 1705, the war against the Emperor was not going well for Guru Singh and his army. They were surrounded by the Emperor's army and trapped in their fort in Anandpur. Soon, the food ran low and the conditions inside the fort became very bad.

One group of forty men decided to leave. They went to Guru Singh and asked his permission. Guru Singh said, "It is your choice to stay or to leave. If you have decided to leave I would like it if you would write your names on a piece of paper saying that I am no longer your Guru." The forty men signed the paper and left the fort that night.

When they reached their home town, these men found that their families were upset and ashamed that they had deserted the Guru. Soon they heard the news that Guru Singh and his men had to flee the fort and were in trouble. The wives of the forty men even offered to go and fight in their place, so the men decided to return and fight.

The forty men found out that Guru Singh had escaped from the fort to a nearby village, but the Emperor's army had surrounded the village and was attacking. When the Guru and his men tried to leave the village, they were chased by the Emperor's army and were trapped near a small lake. Just then the forty men arrived. Together, these forty men helped defeat the Emperor's army and saved Guru Singh's life. But all of the forty men who had returned were killed.

Just before he died, one of the men said to the Guru, "I have only one request. Please, tear up that piece of paper on which I, with my other friends, wrote our names when we deserted you. Just say that you have forgiven us." Guru Singh took out the paper and tore it up and forgave all of the men.

▼ This procession is in honour of the Forty Immortals.

Today, these forty Sikhs are called the Chali Mukte – the 'FORTY IMMORTALS'. It so happened that they were CREMATED on the day of the Hindu holiday of Lohri. So, after this time, the Sikhs changed the name of the holiday to Maghi (after the month of Magh) and celebrated it as a time to remember the Forty Immortals.

Maghi celebrations

Maghi is celebrated in gurdwaras around the world. The Guru Granth Sahib is recited cover to cover. This is called an AKHAND PATH. It takes around 48 hours and many people take turns, with each person reciting for a few hours.

There may also be special worship services where people can hear religious talks about the meaning of sacrifice, and hear stories and poems about the Forty Immortals.

The largest celebration happens in Punjab, near the town of Mukstar. This is where the final battle was fought and where the Forty Immortals died while fighting to save Guru Singh.

During Maghi there is a big fair in Mukstar. There are also many shrines in Mukstar that are dedicated to the Forty Immortals. People travel from far away to worship at the shrines and to swim in the lake near where the Forty Immortals died. This lake is now called The Pool of Liberation.

At the end of the three-day holiday there is a procession which travels from the main shrine to the gurdwara Tibbi Sahib. This gurdwara was sacred to Guru Gobind Singh. At the gurdwara there are worship services dedicated to remembering the Forty Immortals.

▼▶ During the holy day of Maghi, processions and worship services remember the sacrifice that was made by the Forty Immortals, who gave up their lives to save Guru Gobind Singh. This is a solemn time, and a time to remember the importance of sacrifice.

Weblink: www.CurriculumVisions.com

Remembering Gurus

There are many holy days in the Sikh calendar that remember and honour the Sikh Gurus.

Throughout the year, there are many holy days that remember birthdays and other important events in the lives of the Sikh Gurus. These holy days are called **GURUPURABS**.

The most important gurupurabs celebrate the birthdays of Guru Nanak and Guru Gobind Singh, and remember the days that Guru Arjan Dev and Guru Tegh Bahadur died.

Some of the gurupurabs happen on the same dates every year. But others, such as Guru Nanak's gurupurab, move around a little from year to year. This is because some of the gurupurabs are based on the lunar calendar and others are based on the **SOLAR** calendar.

Before the gurupurab

Most gurupurabs are celebrated by reading the entire holy book, the Guru Granth Sahib, nonstop. This is called an akhand path and it finishes on the day of the gurupurab. The reading is done by a team of readers. Each reads for two to three hours.

◀▶During an akhand path the entire Guru Granth Sahib is read nonstop.

Akhand path

The tradition of the **AKHAND PATH** started in India in the mid-18th century, when there were only a few copies of the Guru Granth Sahib. At this time, the Sikhs were at war and it was difficult to worship openly. People would carry copies of the Guru Granth Sahib from place to place and people would gather round to hear readings from the sacred text before it was moved on to be read to other groups of Sikhs.

In India, there may also be a procession, called a prabhat pheris, each day for three weeks before the gurupurab. Early each morning, worshippers walk through their neighbourhoods singing hymns. As the procession passes each house, people offer sweets and tea to the worshippers.

The day of the gurupurab

On the day of the gurupurab, worship may begin early in the morning with the singing of prayers and hymns from the Guru Granth Sahib.

After this the Guru Granth Sahib is carried in a procession, called a **NAGAR KIRTAN**, on a float decorated with flowers. The procession travels through the neighbourhood around the gurdwara. It is led by five men who represent the Panj Piares, the first five baptised Sikhs. Each of these men carries a Sikh flag.

During the procession, local bands play religious music and hymns are sung. The procession may also include people performing mock battles with traditional weapons.

There is also an outdoor langar and everyone who is present is offered sweets and other foods.

After the procession, Sikhs might visit gurdwaras where special programmes are arranged and religious songs called kirtans are sung. There may also be lectures or talks on Sikhism and recitation of poems in praise of the Guru.

▶ This nagar kirtan is in Southall, London.

Some important gurupurabs

Sikhs may hold gurupurabs on any or all of these dates. Not every gurdwara holds a gurupurab on every one of these dates. Since 1999 these dates have been fixed and always fall on the following days, although other holidays move around the calendar.

Guru Nanak Dev Ji

Birthday celebration April 14.

Remembrance of his death September 22.

(Sikhs believe that Guru Nanak was born as a Guru, so they do not celebrate a day on which he became Guru.)

This is one of the biggest gurupurabs of the year. Guru Nanak was the founder of the Sikh faith and the first Sikh Guru. He was born on October 20, 1469, but his gurupurab is celebrated on the day of the Full Moon in the month of Katik. This is usually in November.

Sikhs from all over the world gather at the Guru's birthplace in Punjab to worship at the gurdwara there.

The Sikhs believe that Guru Nanak brought enlightenment to the world, so the festival is also called Prakash Utsav, the festival of light.

Guru Gobind Singh Ji

Birthday celebration January 5.

Celebration of becoming Guru November 24.

Remembrance of his death October 21.

Guru Gobind Singh, the tenth Guru, was born at Patna Sahib on December 22, 1666. His gurupurab is celebrated on January 5.

Guru Granth Sahib

Completion of Granth Sahib Ji August 16.

The Sikh Holy scripture also has a gurupurab. This gurupurab celebrates the day that the Guru Granth Sahib was first placed in the Golden Temple in Amritsar. It is on September 1.

Guru Tegh Bahadur Ji

Birthday celebration April 18.

Celebration of becoming Guru April 16.

Remembrance of his death November 24.

Guru Tegh Bahadur was the ninth of the ten Sikh Gurus. He was born in Amritsar, India. His gurupurab remembers his death.

During Guru Bahadur's lifetime, the Moghul Emperor Aurangzeb tried to force everyone to convert to Islam. He destroyed Hindu and Sikh temples and many people who refused to convert were put into jail.

Guru Tegh Bahadur refused to convert to Islam and so in 1675 he was jailed and the Emperor ordered him to be beheaded. The site of his execution, in Delhi, was later turned into a large gurdwara.

Guru Bahadur's gurupurab is celebrated on November 24. It is also a time to remember the importance of religious freedom for everyone.

Guru Angad Dev Ji

Birthday celebration April 18.

Celebration of becoming Guru September 18.

Remembrance of his death April 16.

Guru Arjan Dev's gurupurab remembers the day he died. Guru Arjan Dev was killed in 1606.

The Moghul Emperor Jahangir had ordered Guru Arjan to change the Sikh holy scripture by removing all Hindu and Muslim words and names from it. Guru Arjan refused to do this and so the emperor ordered him to be tortured and burnt to death with oil and hot sand. The gurupurab that remembers this event is celebrated on June 16 each year.

In Lahore, India, many people visit the Guru's tomb on this day. During the processions, Sikhs hand out cold drinks to people in the street, so that no one has to suffer thirst the way the Guru did before he died.

Khalsa

Creation of the Khalsa April 14.

Guru Amar Das Ji

Birthday celebration May 23.

Celebration of becoming Guru April 16.

Remembrance of his death September 16.

Guru Ram Das Ji

Birthday celebration October 9.

Celebration of becoming Guru September 16.

Remembrance of his death September 16.

Guru Har Krishnan Ji

Birthday celebration 23 July.

Celebration of becoming Guru 20 October.

Remembrance of his death 16 April.

Guru Arjan Dev Ji

Birthday celebration May 2.

Celebration of becoming Guru September 16.

Remembrance of his death June 16.

Guru Hargobind Ji

Birthday celebration July 5.

Celebration of becoming Guru June 11.

Remembrance of his death March 19.

Guru Har Rai Ji

Birthday celebration January 31.

Celebration of becoming Guru March 14.

Remembrance of his death 20 October.

Weblink: www.CurriculumVisions.com

Index

Curriculum Visions

Curriculum Visions is a registered trademark of Atlantic Europe Publishing Company Ltd.

◆ *Atlantic Europe Publishing*

First published in 2007 by Atlantic Europe Publishing Company Ltd Copyright © 2007 Earthscape

The right of Lisa Magloff to be identified as the author of this work has been asserted by her in accordance with the Copyright, Designs and Patents Act 1988.

All rights reserved. No part of this publication may be reproduced, stored in a retrieval system, or transmitted in any form or by any means, electronic, mechanical, photocopying, recording or otherwise, without prior permission of the Publisher and the copyright holder.

Author
Lisa Magloff, MA

Religious Adviser
Hardeep Sarhota

Senior Designer
Adele Humphries, BA

Acknowledgements
The publishers would like to thank the following for their help and advice: Sri Guru Singh Sabha gurdwara, London, and the Sikh community of Southall.

Photographs
The Earthscape Picture Library, except: (c=centre, t=top, b=bottom, l=left, r=right) pages 8–9, 20 *Alamy*; pages 19, 30–31 *Art Directors/TRIP*; pages 16–17, 17tr, 18 *ShutterStock*; pages 12b, 14t, 15 *UK Student Life*.

Illustrations
David Woodroffe

Designed and produced by
Earthscape

Printed in China by
WKT Company Ltd

Sikh holy days
– *Curriculum Visions*
A CIP record for this book is available from the British Library
ISBN: 978 1 86214 508 5

This product is manufactured from sustainable managed forests. For every tree cut down at least one more is planted.

Dedicated Web Site
There's more about other great Curriculum Visions packs and a wealth of supporting information on world religions and other subjects at our dedicated web site:
www.CurriculumVisions.com